1   Open for Business
2   The Southern Banks
6   Qianjiang CBD, Garden of Eden
10   Legend of Alibaba
13   Jack Ma on Hangzhou
16   Business Advice From Those in the Know
24   Shopping and Saving
25   The Silk Culture in Hangzhou
31   The Crafts of Hangzhou
35   Tea From the Dragon
39   Know Where to Shop
44   Hangzhou Nights
49   Appendix

专业外教　英文朗读
扫码免费收听全书

更多英文原创中国故事
来《汉语世界》畅读
theworldofchinese.com

注册网站，点击右上角 subscribe 订阅，
输入优惠码 HANGZHOU
享受读者专属折扣！

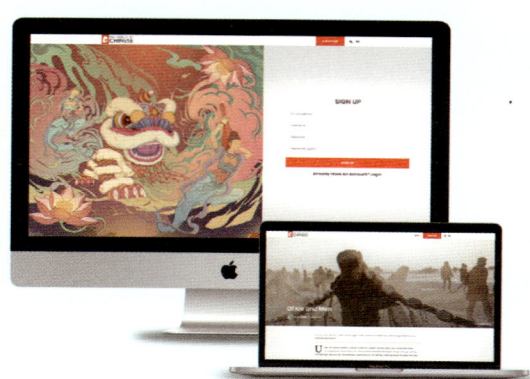

Open for Business

Much of Hangzhou's reputation comes from its history and natural beauty, but that status is changing. Indeed, for many, including billionaire e-commerce mogul Jack Ma, Hangzhou represents a changing of the tides for China. Be it tech, logistics, education, or service, the booming economy of Hangzhou is a place to watch when it comes to the wealth of the world. For entrepreneurs wanting their spot in the Chinese market, Hangzhou is a city that's worth their effort to make the fortune.

billionaire
亿万富翁

mogul
富豪

change of the tides
潮流变幻

logistics
物流

The Southern Banks

Every summer, swimming enthusiasts taking part in the Qiantang River crossing competition jump into the water near the iconic "City Balcony" on the northern banks of the Qiantang River.

An observer watching from the north can see the impressive skyline of the Binjiang high-tech entrepreneurial hub. The 280-meter-tall twin towers, located at the western tip of the new Hangzhou Airport Expressway, will rise to represent the future height of Hangzhou.

Called the "Gate of Wisdom," the twin structure's truly dramatic presentation of the Chinese character "门" suggests the idea of a gateway. The towers will be the centerpiece of the Hangzhou Internet of Things Town that is already a booming industrial base and home to a dozen industry leaders.

For the older generation in Hangzhou, the geographical conception of the city does not include the southern banks of the Qiantang River. The turn of the century, however, saw Hangzhou enter the "Age of the Qiantang River" and with it, the rise of a brand-new Binjiang

District on the southern shores. This new extension of the modern city has not only turned this part of Hangzhou into an entrepreneurial powerhouse but also brought Hangzhounese closer to the scenic beauty and cultural grandeur of the "mother river" of Zhejiang Province. Officially known as the Hangzhou High-Tech Industrial Development Zone, this neat urban district now plays host to a galaxy of apartments, hotels, and headquarters of multinational corporations, reshaping the general view of what the "City of Hangzhou" really is.

After two decades of vigorous development, today's Binjiang is a paradise for entrepreneurial dreamers. There is a high concentration of top-level residential blocks, the city's only international school (Hangzhou International School), Zhejiang Chinese Medicine University, a cluster of industrial leaders including the Binjiang base of China's e-commerce star, Alibaba Group, and many hot cultural and leisure places. Binjiang has become an ideal settlement for locals and resident foreigners alike.

Boasting a gorgeous view of the river and the metropolitan skyline of the north banks that embrace the old Hangzhou

powerhouse
动力源

grandeur
壮观

vigorous
充满活力的

paradise
乐园

metropolitan
大都市的

angler
垂钓者

dub
授予称号

consecutive
连续的

LOHAS, Lifestyles of Health and Sustainability
"乐活",健康和可持续的生活方式

proper, Wentao Road has what promises to be China's longest and most beautiful street and is a favorite hangout for the city's angler community. The road has been used as a key running section of the yearly Hangzhou Marathon, dubbed "World's Most Beautiful Marathon" for two consecutive years. Future development of this scenic riverside belt aims to build a leisure hub for all Binjiang residents to enjoy a LOHAS existence in the strictest sense of the word.

Qiantang River Bridge

When Chinese engineer Mao Yisheng and his team announced their intention to build a bridge over the Qiantang River in 1934, the idea was dismissed by many as mission impossible. However, it took the team only three years to unveil the groundbreaking structure. Unfortunately, the newly-built bridge had to be bombed as part of the anti-Japanese invasion strategy on December 23, 1937. The reconstruction was completed in 1953. The 1,453-meter dual-purpose road-and-railway bridge is one of the two masterpieces of Mao Yisheng, the forefather of modern bridge engineering in China. The bridge has been serving the city for more than 70 years.

unveil
使公之于众

forefather
前辈

Qianjiang CBD, Garden of Eden

Eden
伊甸园

aspire
致力于

Hangzhou's new Qianjiang Central Business District (CBD) aspires to be a kind of Eden for new businesses. It acts as Hangzhou's equivalent to the Lujiazui financial quarter in Shanghai or Central in Hong Kong. The Qianjiang CBD's key distinction is its architecture, urban planning, and garden-like quality. Three major buildings form the core of the CBD: Hangzhou Citizen Center, Hangzhou International Conference Center, and the Hangzhou Grand Theatre.

Hangzhou Citizen Center is defined by six skyscrapers that form a giant circle, linked with connected glass causeways in the sky. Staying true to Chinese culture, the grand theatre and the conference center are shaped like the moon and the sun, facing each other across the Wave Culture Center. This skyline is also marked with a giant golden sphere for luck and prosperity at the conference center.

For those with a burning creative spirit, the area also hosts a world-class library. The new Hangzhou Library has over five floors at 43,680 square meters and a storage capacity for two million books. Foreigners can access the collections with their passport and a small fee, or free of charge if the patron can provide proof of employment in Hangzhou.

Promising Future

China's State Council approved Hangzhou's 2016 to 2020 master-plan, which stresses the special balance of nature, history, culture, rural life, and urbanism that defines Hangzhou. Environmental and UNESCO heritage protection is of paramount importance in this plan, with height limitations for buildings on West Lake, Qiantang River, Grand Canal, Xixi Wetlands, Qinghefang Historical and Cultural Block, and other Southern Song Dynasty period buildings. All of these will enhance the new CBD as it matures and leads the city's growth while preserving the past. Long-term development plans also include offices, hotels, shopping malls, and luxury residential neighborhoods in the Wangjiang and Canal sub-districts.

of paramount importance
至关重要

杭州一瞥：厚登时代

Hangzhou Olympic Sports Center on the southern bank of the Qiantang River

MODERN HANGZHOU

Legend of Alibaba

Jumpin' Jack Flash

obscure 不知名的

nimble 机敏的

chicken 胆小的

set in motion 使……运转

He went from being an obscure tour guide on the banks of West Lake to the envy of all world banks. Meet Ma Yun, but perhaps you know him better as Jack Ma, Hangzhou's homegrown hero and global ambassador whose companies are changing how the world does business. Born on September 10, 1964, to musician-storyteller parents, the young Ma Yun began making money by showing tourists around his city. For nine years, he would walk to the Hangzhou Hotel—now the Shangri-La—and learn English while showing guests around this fairytale city. Jack was nimble, Jack was quick, and his knowledge of Hangzhou's history and culture was his magic trick. Being no chicken, Jack went on to study at Hangzhou Normal University and the local trade offices.

On a fateful trade trip to Seattle in 1995, he used the internet for the first time and typed in "beer." Seeing there was no Chinese beer listed and virtually no information on China, he set his ideas in motion to make a website about China. He returned home and started making Chinese websites with the company "China Yellow Pages." In 1999, he launched Alibaba with 17 friends in his little Hangzhou flat. No one in the world could have known it then, but they were living and creating a new Hangzhou legend.

Jack and his merry band of webmakers, like Ali Baba and the 40 Thieves from the Arabian tale in *A Thousand and One Nights* loved the idea of the magic "Open Sesame." Soon after opening, capital investments to the tune of 25 million USD began pouring into the little net start-up faster than one could say "Open Sesame."

Quickly, the platform began taking Chinese SMEs mainstream with e-commerce ventures such as Taobao Marketplace, Alipay, Alimama, and more, bringing in Yahoo!

By 2014, as the company was about to take its IPO on the New York Stock Exchanges and go supernova as NYSE: BABA, they had nearly 100 million users in over 20 countries with global online transactions exceeding one trillion RMB. The company continued to move at perhaps one of the fastest paces in the world, with ventures into entertainment,

---

to the tune of
高达

SME, Small to Medium Enterprise
中小型企业

venture
冒险事业

IPO, Initial Public Offering
首次公开募股

supernova
超新星

hive 蜂巢	cinema, sports, and beyond. The company's stated 2020 goals are to exceed 72.9 billion USD in annual revenues, but that's all part of the plan.

The Hive

Nestled amidst the Xixi Wetlands region of Hangzhou are the main facilities for the e-commerce empire of Alibaba. This architecture embodies the sort of sci-fi like vision of work and nature that Jack Ma emphasizes as a CEO and philanthropist: harmony of both natural and economic ecosystems with Hangzhou characteristics.

All employees here must take on a character name from one of the novels from Hong Kong writer Louis Cha Leung-yung, popularly known as Jin Yong. Regardless of whether they are new hires or old hats, they are eligible for the company's unique marriage lottery. Every May, Jack Ma marries employees in massive wedding ceremonies. At their peak, Jack married almost 700 at a time.

Sidebar vocabulary:

hive
蜂巢

embody
体现

sci-fi
科幻小说

philanthropist
慈善家

Jack Ma on Hangzhou

I was born in Hangzhou, I grew up in Hangzhou, studied in Hangzhou, and worked in Hangzhou. I started businesses in Hangzhou, my home is in Hangzhou, my colleagues are in Hangzhou, and my dreams are in Hangzhou. Hangzhou gives me sustenance. "Hangzhou Guy" is practically written on my face. This life of mine is in Hangzhou.

Hangzhou is a magical place. The scenery is exquisite. But Hangzhou folks are nicknamed "Iron Heads." We Hangzhou guys are very stubborn.

I like Hangzhou. What other city can compare with it? There is West Lake, there are tea houses. We even have our own card game.

When I was small, I was taught English by Chinese teachers. I felt like that wasn't working, so where could I find myself a teacher? I thought foreigners would be the best English teachers. Starting from age 12 or 13, I hung around at the entrance of the Shangri-La Hotel on Beishan Road by West Lake every day to meet

sustenance
给养

exquisite
精致的

storytelling
评书

Suzhou-style ballad
苏州评弹

steep
浸泡

inspiration
灵感

foreigners, offering myself as their tour guide with the goal of learning English. In nine years' time, I'd gone around every inch of West Lake, and I learned English really well.

Another place I often went to as a child was the Hangzhou tea house, along with my father. We listened to storytelling, to Suzhou-style ballads, to the masters telling of the Three Kingdoms and General Yue Fei. You can say I was steeped in the tea house as I grew up.

Many of the major decisions concerning Alibaba were made in a tea house. The annual West Lake Summits were a sudden inspiration while sitting inside a tea house. It was also inside a tea house by West Lake that we decided to create Taobao.com.

Hangzhou has something that exists nowhere else in the world, and that's a card game called "Three Against One." Nobody outside Hangzhou knows how to play it. It's a Hangzhou specialty.

Hangzhou is the Eden of Alibaba. Without Hangzhou, there is no Alibaba. Alibaba is a "rare flower." This rare flower drew benefits from the

MODERN HANGZHOU

soil of private enterprise. The target of Alibaba's services is those tens of thousands of small businesses. Our mission is to provide a platform so that no business is too difficult to do.

Business Advice From Those in the Know

Company Son

Alibaba's Daniel Draper is in no way related to the Don Draper of *Mad Men* fame, but the two share one thing in common: starring in legendary business roles in heady historical times. Australian Daniel Draper joined Alibaba in 2000, when he was just 22 and fresh out of Mandarin study at Zhejiang University. Back then, China had yet to join the World Trade Organization (WTO) and Alibaba was just a year-old operation. Daniel has been there for Alibaba's meteoric rise and has done so in a variety of roles, from the "Safety and Trust Team" to his current duties handling the public face of the international divisions.

Q: What makes Alibaba a dynamic place to work?

I've actually been at Alibaba pretty much since the beginning. I've seen it grow from a small startup with a big dream to being the leading player in many areas. From the initial start as a B2B trade listings site in 1999, through to growing China's dominant e-commerce platforms

---

heady
兴奋的

meteoric
疾速的

dynamic
有活力的

B2B, Business-to-Business
企业对企业

MODERN HANGZHOU

and online payments, through to innovative fintech, online entertainment, and an ever-growing list of others.

Q: What's it like to work with Jack Ma?

It has been an honor and privilege to work with a guy who has built up these companies that have changed so many aspects of life in China.

Q: Where do you like to go to unwind in Hangzhou?

I guess my best spot for relaxing would be picnicking down by Xianghu Lake with my family, or in one of the areas around the tea fields in the hills to the west of West Lake.

All in the Family

A key division for Alibaba is Europe, where another fresh-faced graduate, Fedor Deichmann, was chosen by senior Alibaba leaders to step up business operations. Based in Berlin, he enjoys flying back to Hangzhou for corporate communion and relaxing by West Lake.

Q: How did you get involved with Alibaba and what excites you about working for them?

I have been very interested in China since the beginning of my college

fintech
金融科技

unwind
放松

stimulant
激励者

macroeconomic
宏观经济的

mount
上升

years. After I graduated, I spent a year studying Chinese in Taiwan, and was lucky to find Alibaba. I joined the company in early 2014, as one of the first foreigners to start Tmall. It's been immensely exciting to be part of a company that is so influential both in the global tech world and in Chinese history as a whole. At Alibaba, we are reinventing the way e-commerce is done through our ecosystem philosophy. At the same time, we are also a significant stimulant in Chinese macroeconomic consumption.

Q: How is interest mounting in Europe about Alibaba? What sort of questions are Europeans raising about it?

Since we went public, Alibaba has become a world-famous company, and for some international companies. Likewise, European companies see Alibaba as a gateway to entering the Chinese market. Therefore, more often than not, our discussions with our many interested potential partners in Europe are not about whether to enter the Chinese market through Alibaba, but how and when to do so. They will often raise questions about the market potential of their products, the costs involved of setting up a storefront operation through our platform, and the kind of marketing services that we can provide to help them amplify their branding. So overall, I would say the reaction from our European clients is very positive, and we are working hard to help make this path to China as smooth and efficient as possible.

Q: What would your advice be to people who want to work for Alibaba?

One of our key values is to "embrace change." I would tell anyone interested in working for Alibaba to be as open-minded and flexible as possible. E-commerce is a very fast-moving industry. The only way to be successful in such an environment is by accepting the changes around you and challenging the routine.

West End Boys

As leaders of a gaggle of young entrepreneurs from Canada, Alex Gale and Lucas Porter-Bakker have networked Hangzhou like no other wholly-owned company ever has.

In 2013, Lucas led a team of ten young Canadians to launch Westgroup, an investment and training center

amplify
增强

a gaggle of
一群

wholly-owned company
独资公司

spike
猛增

incubator
孵化基地

company in Hangzhou. "After a year of registration procedures, we finally got our license and approved name and opened our first English training center. We do basic business English and have several excellent Hangzhou government clients, including over 4,000 from the airport who are trained to welcome guests for the G20," says Lucas, Westgroup's managing director.

Staying focused is of paramount importance to this young group as Hangzhou expands and demand for their English training services spikes. "We're now seeing investment incubators in Hangzhou thanks to Alibaba and creative and tech startups emerging. Way more companies are moving in, real-estate is picking up, and more people around China want to relocate here. This is going to mean more business for us as we are the only training centers of English totally owned and run by native speakers," explains Lucas. In early 2016, Westgroup launched an app called "Goji." "This app allows Chinese university students to send voice messages to American students to practice their English," says Lucas. "The app is a good example of the training and tech opportunities in Hangzhou. It takes work but it's well worth it and we are here for the long run."

From Trade to Tourism

Egyptians Said Abollsaed and Faraned Rasmy Emad stroll along the northern banks of West Lake with bright smiles. "Today is a beautiful day and it inspires me. With all of these people, some are going to get hungry and I want to open an Egyptian restaurant here for them," says Said. His friend and business partner Faraned concurs, "Hangzhou will be very good to open a business for Egyptian food."

The two partners are already established traders in the nearby Yiwu City. Like many traders in Yiwu they have partner offices in Hangzhou.

"I like to come to Hangzhou to relax and enjoy nature… here there are quite a lot of tourist places that can be drawn on the world's map to go to," Said commented. "We could easily run more and more trading businesses here, and we plan to expand into tourism services, not just for Chinese but for tourists from all over the world who come here."

concur
赞同

hail from 来自	
plugged-in 紧跟时代	
instantaneously 即刻	

Plugged In

Hailing from Manchester, United Kingdom, Don Munro is a plugged-in guy—as one might suspect from the CEO and founder of Efergy, a company that manufactures energy monitoring products for the global market place.

Q: What encouraged you to set up Efergy in Hangzhou?

Actually, the main reason is that it's in a perfect location. I also met my business partner here. He was working on a UN project and spotted a gap in the market to supply an electronic display that would allow households to monitor their electricity use instantaneously.

Q: How do you view Hangzhou as a city for foreign entrepreneurs?

It's no coincidence that Hangzhou won the *Forbes Magazine* "Best Cities for Commerce Award" for many years. It's also won the national award for "China's Happiest City" consecutively for 11 years. It's a great technology hub, with the beautiful West Lake in the middle of the city and tea mountains 15 minutes away.

Q: What is your near and long-term view for Hangzhou as a creative and IT hub?

MODERN HANGZHOU

Hangzhou has always been a beautiful place for people to work and relax. However, now the local government is investing in building an infrastructure to take the city forward in the future. This is enticing a lot of new exciting tech companies here. The future is very bright for Hangzhou.

infrastructure
基础设施

entice
吸引

Shopping and Saving

haggle
砍价

If there's one thing visitors do in Hangzhou, it's shopping. From handicrafts lovingly made by careful hands to the most luxurious silk in the finest shops, the city is known for the special care put into its products. For those who want to shop in true Hangzhou style (and don't mind a little bit of haggling), the best part of the Hangzhou shopping scene is in its street markets—where centuries-old streets provide buyers with unique options found nowhere else on earth.

The Silk Culture in Hangzhou

Having been one of the major centers for silk production for centuries, silk runs through the lifeblood of Hangzhou, and you can find a place to buy it on every street corner. Perhaps more important for shoppers is being able to tell the difference between the more than 14 different types of silk. For instance, *chou* is your most common silk; thin and soft, it's often made into dresses, blouses, or night gowns. *Duan* is a little bit thicker. It's smooth if you stroke it from the right direction, and this is because during weaving, one of the crossed threads is always on top. *Duan* is often brocaded and made into an autumn or winter *qipao*.

The most famous, though, is *hangluo*. Using pure silkworm thread and woven in an extremely complex pattern, the fabric is famed for being light and breathable, perfect for a summer *qipao*. *Luo* silk history can be traced all the way back to the Spring and Autumn Period. In the Three Kingdoms Period (220–280), today's Hangzhou area belonged to the Wu Kingdom, whose first lady, Madam Zhao, was famous

---

lifeblood
命脉

chou
绸

duan
缎

brocaded
织成锦缎的

hangluo
杭罗

fabric
织物

luo
罗

Glossary	
luoqun 罗裙	
intangible cultural heritage 非物质文化遗产	
keep an eye out for 留心	
facet 方面	
millennia 一千年	
zhijin 织锦	
textile 纺织品	

for her *luo*-weaving skills. When it came to the Southern Song Dynasty, Lin'an fashion dictated that ladies would wear full-length dresses, mostly made of *luo* silk, coining the term *luoqun*, or "*luo* dress." Long gowns with loose sleeves made of *luo* were equally popular with the gentlemen of the age. Until recent history, *hangluo* was reserved for the rich and powerful—1930s Shanghai tycoons needed at least a few white *hangluo* gowns in their closets to even be considered well-dressed. The ancient technique of making *hangluo* was recognized as UNESCO intangible cultural heritage in 2009, and if you're looking to take home a bit of this culture, keep an eye out for the brand Fuxing Hangluo, produced by Fuxing Silk Factory.

Silk dyeing has been an important facet of silk production for millennia. The former Hangzhou Silk Printing and Dyeing Factory, now known as Xidebao, is a renowned silk brand specializing in hand-dyeing silk.

But, if you're looking for decoration rather than fashion, the local *zhijin*, or brocade, will definitely satisfy. Named after the patriotic textile businessman Du Jinsheng, active in the 1920s to 1930s, this silk brocade is a relatively modern textile design. Drawing inspiration from the beautiful natural scenery around Hangzhou, native-born Du invented the art of landscape "painting" on silk, and hand-woven the first of its kind based on the local attraction, Nine Brooks and Eighteen Streams. In 1926, their brocade even won the gold prize at the Philadelphia World Expo.

As far as where to go, you can find everything you need in China Silk Town, the biggest silk wholesale and retail market in the country, with more than 600 silk enterprises dealing in a wide variety of pure silk fabrics, garments, handicraft articles, scarves, and ties. On Hefang Street, one of the most famous historic streets in the city, you will find brand names like Silk Depot and many other independent shops full of innovative silk souvenirs and handicrafts. Of course, you can also go to department stores like the Hangzhou Tower or Intime Department Store for guaranteed quality.

wholesale
批发

souvenir
纪念品

▍Origin of Silk

Legends attribute the invention of silk to Leizu, the empress of the Yellow Emperor, a legendary sovereign. It was said that when Leizu was drinking a cup of tea, a silkworm cocoon fell into her cup. Then, because of the heat, a fine thread started to separate itself from the silkworm cocoon, and Leizu found that she could unwind this soft thread around her finger. She persuaded her husband to give her a grove of mulberry trees, where she could raise the worms and harvest their cocoons.

---

sovereign
统治者

cocoon
蚕茧

unwind
解开

mulberry tree
桑树

China National Silk Museum

China National Silk Museum is one of the first state-level museums in China, where you'll find 9,000 square meters of displays divided into several galleries with a 40,000-square-meter southern Chinese-style garden.

The first Silk Road Gallery will take you on a journey through the annals of Chinese silk both historically and geographically. The earliest preserved silks from the Qianshanyang Site, Huzhou (c.2200 BCE) and the earliest pattern loom model from Laoguanshan Han Dynasty Tomb in Chengdu (c.100 BCE) can be found on display in this gallery. More amazing silk textiles from the Silk Road—which include both colorful woven silks from northwest China from the third to 10th centuries as well as painted and embroidered silks from Europe, mostly from the 18th to 19th centuries—will wow silk lovers from around the globe.

For more information on how silk is made, visitors can move into the Sericulture and Weaving Galleries. The process of sericulture and silk

---

gallery
画廊

annal
记录

loom
织布机

embroidered
刺绣的

sericulture
蚕丝业

craftsmanship
工艺

boutique
精品店

craftsmanship in China is listed as UNESCO intangible cultural heritage—including the entire process of mulberry planting, silkworm raising, cocoon cultivation, dyeing, weaving, and embroidery. Lovers of style will enjoy the Fashion Gallery, which is dedicated to contemporary costumes, from the Chinese fashion of the 20th century to 400 years of Western fashion. For shopping, you can also visit the Jingluntang silk boutique located in the basement of the Fashion Gallery for high-quality designer silk products, or head to the basement of the Silk Road Gallery for local silk products.

The Crafts of Hangzhou

Wang Xing Ji Fans

Established in 1875 by Wang Xingzhai and his wife Chen, who was a skilled fan-maker, the Wang Xing Ji brand of fans won instant popularity because of their refined choice of materials, delicate craftsmanship, and unique style. In 1930, having studied nearly all fans produced abroad, Wang came up with a new fan design. He selected sandalwood for the ribs and covered them with fine silks painted with the scenes of West Lake. After 1949, Wang Xing Ji continued to develop and expand. At present, the brand produces 11 types of fans in more than 300 variations. With elegant carvings and a long-lasting fragrance, sandalwood fans are their most prized products.

West Lake Silk Umbrella

Combining the native-grown bamboo and locally woven silk, the first West Lake silk umbrella was made in the 1930s by craftsman Zhu Zhenfei in Du Jinsheng's silk brocade factory. Thin, breathable, and easily folded, the silk

sandalwood
檀香木

rib
扇骨

umbrella features patterns of West Lake scenery, flowers, birds, and various other traditional designs.

Copper Sculpture

Back in the Shang Dynasty (1600 BCE – 1046 BCE), the ancient Chinese created large numbers of bronze vessels covered with intricate decorations for use in sacrificial rituals. Thousands of years later, this art survives. While in Hangzhou, be sure to check out Zhu Bingren Bronze Art Museum, where visitors can appreciate calligraphy, paintings, frescos, and Buddha figures in the finest copper. With an area of around 3,000 square meters, the museum is entirely made of copper—including doors, windows, pillars, and furniture, totaling 65 tons. Zhu Bingren, after whom the museum is named, is known as the "Father of Modern Bronze and Copper Art in China." Hangzhou copper sculpture, as well as the "Copper Art of the Zhu Family," have been recognized as a national intangible cultural heritage.

---

copper
铜

bronze vessel
青铜器

intricate
复杂的

Hang Embroidery

Often referred to as "Hang embroidery," Hangzhou's special brand of embroidery has its roots in the Southern Song Dynasty, divided into two parts: court embroidery and folk embroidery. With many different methods and a unique style, most patterns stem from stylizations of folk life and traditions. Also, as Hangzhou was a city of rich religious tradition, religious works played their part. *The Lotus Sutra*, made by two female Buddhists from 1355 to 1361 and considered a masterpiece, can be found in the Shanghai Museum today. Due to the prosperity of the silk industry, from the Song Dynasty to the Ming and Qing dynasties, Hangzhou was the main producer of embroidery for the nation.

Kong Feng Chun Face Powder

Specializing in "goose egg powder," referring to the shape of the pressed powder rather than its ingredients, this 19th century cosmetic brand was said to have been on the dressing table of the Empress Dowager Cixi herself. The shop, located in Qinghefang, was extremely popular in the 1920s and

---

Hang embroidery
杭绣

stem from
起源于

stylization
仿效

goose egg powder
鹅蛋粉

cosmetic
化妆品

dressing table
梳妆台

pre-industrial 工业化以前的	1930s. Though Hangzhou women are faced with increasingly modern choices when it comes to cosmetics, the century-old brand still holds a special place in their hearts.
forge 锻造	
clippers 剪刀	**Zhang Xiaoquan Scissors**
wrought iron 熟铁	Zhang Xiaoquan was a great pre-industrial craftsman, who greatly improved scissors' quality by applying new technology in the forging process. Zhang's process for making the perfect pair of clippers involved as many as 72 different steps. The most difficult step of all is setting steel in wrought iron to be hammered repeatedly, then ground with mud bricks to give it a sharp edge. In 2006, the forging techniques of Zhang Xiaoquan scissors were added to the national intangible cultural heritage list.
grind 研磨	

Tea From the Dragon

Hangzhou people are very proud of their West Lake Longjing, considered one of the finest types of green tea in China, known for its emerald color, sparrow tongue-shaped leaves, bittersweet taste, and rich aroma. Its name, "Longjing," or "Dragon Well," was originally the name of a wellspring located in a village southwest of West Lake. Tea has been cultivated in this area for at least 1,500 years and has been closely linked to Buddhism since the very beginning. It was believed that the fifth century scholar Xie Lingyun was the first person to bring the plant here from the Chan Buddhism holy ground Tiantai Mountain while he was at Tianzhu Temple to translate Buddhist scriptures from Sanskrit to Chinese. It became customary for temples to grow tea on their grounds.

There are a few tea houses you simply can't miss in Hangzhou. The most well-known teahouse is Hu Pan Ju Teahouse located in the northeastern shore of West Lake. It provides the best Longjing tea, a large variety of snacks, tea ceremonies, and an amazing view of West Lake.

emerald
翠绿色

aroma
芳香

wellspring
泉源

scripture
经文

Sanskrit
梵文

tea ceremony
茶道

cuisine
美食

antique
古老的

funnel
茶壶嘴

Another noted chain tea house is Qingteng Teahouse, featuring tasteful decoration and a great selection of tea and cuisine. If you are in the antique Hefang Street area, Tai Chi Teahouse should be your first choice. It features waiters and waitresses dressed in traditional Chinese clothes pouring tea from long funnels of big copper teapots.

Hupao Spring

To brew the perfect cup of tea, water is as important as the tea leaves. Hangzhou locals will tell you that a good cup of Longjing should be brewed with water from Hupao Spring a few kilometers south of West Lake. The name of the spring is taken from a legend in which a Tang Dynasty monk named Chan Master Huanzhong lived in the area for its extraordinary beauty but couldn't find a water source. Just as he was about to move, he had a dream in which an immortal told him: "There's a spring in Nanyue Mountain, and I will send two tigers to move it here." The next day, the monk saw two tigers digging in the earth to make a den and clear spring water gushed from the ground.

brew
沏

den
穴

gush
涌

Chenghuang Pavilion

stunning
极漂亮的

If you find yourself on the Hefang Street in need of a stunning view and tea, then head for one of the most iconic images of the Hangzhou skyline, the 41-meter Chenghuang Pavilion at Wushan Hill.

Inside the seven-storey pavilion is an exhibition hall with displays of tea culture, dragon boat racing, and stories from history. On the third to the sixth floor, visitors can grab a cup of tea while appreciating the view.

Know Where to Shop

Made for Mall Rats

The city has a fascinating array of goods to offer, ranging from international imported brands to similar, cheaper domestic versions to traditional wares that represent the unique culture of Hangzhou. For a leisurely day of window shopping and a taste of Hangzhou's modern pulse, you'll need to remember three places: Yan'an Road, the lakeside Hubin Road, and the newly-developed Public Services Center where The MIXC Mall is situated.

The lakeside Hubin Road boasts the city's most luxurious department stores, Jiefang Road Department Store, Lakeside Deluxe Street, "in77," featuring an Apple flagship store, and Lixing Mall, which has one of the largest MUJI marketplaces in eastern China. A lakeside promenade is enough to take in the breathtaking beauty of West Lake while enjoying the newest trends of high fashion to the fullest.

The city's INTIME corporation operates a dozen stores all in prime downtown locations. The lakeside

array
大量

window shopping
只看不买

promenade
步行区

cater to
迎合

benchmark
衡量基准

top-notch
顶级的

ice rink
溜冰场

commercial agglomeration
商圈

branch is a newly renovated place with a surprising offering of around 600 fashion brands that caters to the needs of white-collar workers and young families.

Hangzhou Tower, headquartered at the northern end of the Yan'an Road CBD, is a big mall that also serves as the city's fashion benchmark, with a lot of international luxury fashion brands, fancy restaurants, and cafes and a top-notch supermarket.

The luxurious side of Hangzhou can also be sampled at The MIXC Mall, a beloved fashion icon that guarantees the ultimate shopping sensation in a sea of international brands and even includes a stylish ice rink. In Hangzhou, Starbucks fans have more than 50 locations across the city to grab a coffee.

In the near future, Wulin Square—or "the heart of Hangzhou"—will gain a massive landmark called Hangzhou Center, a stylish commercial agglomeration that promises the people of Hangzhou the best shopping experience ever.

Wushan Night Market

For the more adventurous, thrifty, and savvy, Hangzhou also has its share of day and night markets. A taste of culture and possibly some hidden treasures can be found in the city's numerous fashion and antique markets—the Wushan Night Market is a must-try.

Confusingly, the name Wushan Night Market has little to do with the city's iconic Wushan Square. It is an ideal place for bargain hunters and a favorite place for the city's street-fashion insiders as well as first-timers in Hangzhou. The narrow streets are packed with booths selling antiques, traditional Chinese artifacts, silk items and more. Most of the booth owners are surprisingly bilingual. Part of the fun is walking through the crowds to enjoy the oddity and novelty of the goods while sharing the hot passion of the booth owners as they interact with picky bargainers.

Sijiqing Clothes Market

Shopping in Hangzhou can also be a gold rush-style experience. At four o'clock every morning throughout the year, the early birds at Hangzhou's Sijiqing Clothes Market are seeking the

---

thrifty
节俭的

savvy
懂行的

antique market
古玩市场

booth
摊位

oddity
奇特

novelty
新奇

picky
挑剔的

rooky
新手

discerning eye
敏锐的眼光

labyrinth
迷宫

authentic
正宗的

best worms of the day. Founded in 1989, Sijiqing is one of the busiest clothing wholesale markets in Zhejiang. Located near the entrance of the Qianjiang No.3 Bridge, the extensive agglomeration that dominates this densely-populated area has been continuously expanded over the past decade, now composed of a dozen markets catering to different needs and budgets.

Sijiqing is not for rookies. It takes some solid knowledge and discerning eyes to make the shopping experience a rewarding one.

Traditional and Fusion

Venturing into the back streets and through the lakeside labyrinth that blends into the Huancheng West Road and Wulin Road in downtown Hangzhou proper can also be a surprisingly rewarding experience.

The Southern Song Imperial Street and the two historical streets, Gaoyin and Hefang in the Wushan Square neighborhood, are worth exploring if you are on the hunt for a bite of the more authentic flavors of Hangzhou.

On one side of the Wulin Road, one

can find the chic Queen's Park complex to relax. The homey decoration of this adorable complex is home to a fine collection of cafes and restaurants and ensures signature Jiangnan-style comfort and elegance, making the venues here perfect for private functions and business parties alike.

Tucked away on the third floor of the complex's centerpiece, Long Tang Li—a household-name chain, much like Grandma's Kitchen and Green Tea—works hard to blend modernity with local tradition, offering a host of innovative Hangzhou favorites and Sichuan/Hunan specialties. The centerpiece of Queen's Park also includes a boutique hotel.

chic
别致的

venue
场馆

function
宴会

tuck away
隐藏

household-name
家喻户晓的

Hangzhou Nights

twilight
暮光

hotspot
热点

plug the gap
填补空白

While it's true that Hangzhou can't compete with the bright lights of Shanghai's or Beijing's nightlife scene, the city has more than enough options to keep you occupied in those magical twilight hours. Hangzhou has an increasingly diverse array of nightlife options that cater to their diverse army of visitors, residents, and guests.

If people-watching is more your game, then a trip to Wulin Road's trendy cafe-and-restaurant hotspot Queen's Park is certainly worth an hour or two of your time. Here you can sip beer from Me Too Cafe's outdoor seating terrace. Also located on Queen's Park is a huge branch of Maan Coffee, a chain coffeehouse that specializes in coffee, waffles, assorted sandwiches, and delicious desserts.

With a new 800-person capacity, MAO Livehouse opening its doors to Hangzhou's growing army of live music fans. In addition, two venues in particular have been doing their best to plug the gaps and, in their own special way, both 9 Club and Loopy Live are fantastic live music venues, featuring craft and imported beers as well as Western food and a wide range of hopeful musicians.

Spread out over hundreds of square meters, 9 Club is a hip, much-loved venue that somehow manages to work as a kind of a pool hall, live house, bar, and club hybrid. Moreover, it's one of the city's best live music hotspots.

Another choice is Hangzhou's premier jazz club JZ Club, which is located near Nanshan Road. Spread out over three floors but comfortable and intimate throughout, JZ Club attracts some of the best jazz artists to set foot in the mainland, and its classy layout is the ideal setting in which to enjoy some fine music and sip on some grade-A whisky while you're at it.

After a hard day's work, you could head to Wade's Bar & Grill, a spacious third-floor sports bar that instantly became a citywide favorite. Wade's serves up hearty Western food such as pizza, pasta, burgers, fajitas—plus some Asian dishes. Complete with an excellent pool table, a ventilation system that somehow manages to keep both smokers and non-smokers happy, great staff, tasty food, and a large, well-stocked bar,

---

hip
风行一时

pool hall
台球房

hybrid
混合体

fajita
墨西哥铁板烧

ventilation system
通风系统

hunker down in 窝在那	Wade's is the kind of place where you want to hunker down in and spend the night.
conspire 谋求	If you'd rather keep the night moving, a short taxi ride to Nanshan Road's Eudora Station would be a good next stop. The rooftop terrace, great cocktails, and generous happy hour have all conspired to make this pub a firm Hangzhou expat favorite. Eudora usually hosts live music on weekend nights, when the atmosphere can get carnival-esque. And its Sunday brunch buffet is something of a Hangzhou institution.
expat 外国人	
carnival-esque 狂欢	
institution 习俗	
rustic 乡村气息的	If that's not really your cup of (green) tea, then perhaps you can take a cab to Shuguang Road, also known as Bar Street, where you will find a pack of lively bars and rustic pubs that won't disappoint.
tried-and-tested 经过验证的	
bar crawl 串酒吧	You Too Bar features loud, live music from rocking local bands, and is a firm local favorite and a good place to liven things up. Further along Shuguang Road, there is a group of tried-and-tested bars that ought to serve as a good conclusion to this leg of your epic Hangzhou bar crawl. A short walk from there, you will see two bars that have seen more action than a Michael Bay movie starring Jason

Statham. Old Captain Lounge Bar and Traveller Bar are not only ideally positioned fairly close to one another, but they are fine alehouses to boot. Serving as the backdrop to countless long and woozy nights in the city, Old Captain Lounge Bar and Traveller Bar are good places to get some serious, late-night drinking done.

If the crowded dance floors of the city leave you feeling cold, then maybe the KTV booth is more your thing. Although karaoke has been a popular pastime all over the world for years, Chinese KTV revolves around private booths that typically hold up to 10 to 15 people, you are with a select group of friends instead.

Probably the most popular KTV venue in town is Mago KTV, a melodic funhouse that boasts two prime locations in the city's downtown core; one is located near some of Hangzhou's most popular bars and watering holes. They have a pretty decent selection of English language numbers—including songs by contemporary artists like the Killers and classics from The Beatles, Michael Jackson, and Madonna.

Pure K has an altogether dark tone throughout its booths, with dark

alehouses
酒馆

to boot
除此之外

woozy
微醉的

watering hole
酒吧

wood, rich leather, and loud wallpaper dominant throughout. It is popular amongst Hangzhou's trendy set. Thanks to its central location, the venue feels like it's in the eye of the city's quickening nightlife storm.

Truth be told, you can pretty much walk into most of the city's KTV venues, such as INLOVE KTV or V-SHOW, and get exactly what you are looking for. There are few better ways to end a night out than with a microphone in your hand.

Appendix

Place Names 地名机构名对照表

9 Club 酒球会

Alibaba Group 阿里巴巴集团

Alibaba Group's Binjiang campus
阿里巴巴滨江园区

Alibaba Group's Xixi campus
阿里巴巴西溪园区

Binjiang District 滨江区

Canal Sub-District 运河街道

Central 中环

Chenghuang Pavilion 城隍阁

China National Silk Museum
中国丝绸博物馆

China Silk Town 中国丝绸城

City Balcony 城市阳台

Eudora Station 亿多瑞站

Fuxing Silk Factory 福兴丝绸厂

Gate of Wisdom 智慧之门

Grandma's Kitchen 外婆家

Green Tea 绿茶

Hangzhou Center 杭州中心

Hangzhou Grand Theatre 杭州大剧院

Hangzhou High-Tech Industrial Development Zone
杭州高新技术产业开发区

Hangzhou Hotel 杭州饭店

Hangzhou International Conference Center 杭州国际会议中心

Hangzhou International School
杭州国际学校

Hangzhou Internet of Things Town
杭州物联网小镇

Hangzhou Library 杭州图书馆

Hangzhou Normal University
杭州师范大学

Hangzhou Citizen Center
杭州市民中心

Hangzhou Shangri-La Hotel
杭州香格里拉饭店

Hangzhou Silk Printing and Dyeing Factory 杭州丝绸印染厂

Hangzhou Tower 杭州大厦

Hefang Street 河坊街

Hu Pan Ju Teahouse
湖畔居茶楼

Hupao Spring 虎跑泉

Huzhou 湖州

in77 湖滨银泰

INLOVE KTV 银乐迪

Intime Department Store 银泰百货

Jiefang Road Department Store
解百购物广场

Jingluntang 经纶堂

JZ Club 黄楼酒吧

Laoguanshan Han Dynasty Tomb 老官山汉墓

Lakeside Deluxe Street 湖滨国际名品街

Lin'an 临安

Lixing Mall 利星名品广场

Long Tang Li 弄堂里

Longjing (Dragon Well) 龙井

Lujiazui 陆家嘴

Maan Coffee 漫咖啡

Mago KTV 嘜歌

Me Too Cafe 蜜桃咖啡

Nanyue Mountain (Hengshan Mountain) 南岳 (衡山)

New York Stock Exchanges 纽约证券交易所

Nine Brooks and Eighteen Streams 九溪十八涧

Old Captain Lounge Bar 老船长酒吧

Pure K 纯K

Qianjiang Central Business District (CBD) 钱江中心商务区

Qianshanyang Site 钱山漾遗址

Qiantang River 钱塘江

Qiantang River Bridge 钱塘江大桥

Qingteng Teahouse 青藤茶馆

Qinghefang Historical and Cultural Block 清河坊历史文化街区

Queen's Park 皇后公园

Shanghai Museum 上海博物馆

Sijiqing Clothes Market 四季青服装市场

Silk Depot 丝瑞宝

Southern Song Imperial Street 南宋御街

Tai Chi Teahouse 太极茶道苑

The Grand Canal 大运河

The MIXC Mall 万象城

Tiantai Mountain 天台山

Tianzhu Temple 天竺寺

Traveller Bar 旅行者酒吧

UNESCO 联合国科教文组织

Wade's Bar & Grill 味德西餐酒吧

Wangjiang Sub-District 望江街道

Wave Culture Center 波浪文化城

West Lake 西湖

World Trade Organization (WTO) 世界贸易组织

Wu Kingdom 吴国 (古)

Wulin Square 武林广场

Wushan Hill 吴山

Wushan Night Market 吴山夜市

Wushan Square 吴山广场

Xianghu Lake 湘湖

Xixi Wetlands 西溪湿地

Yiwu City 义乌市

Zhejiang Chinese Medical University
浙江中医药大学

Zhejiang University 浙江大学

Zhu Bingren Bronze Art Museum
朱炳仁铜雕艺术博物馆

Names of Important Figures 人名对照表

Chan Master Huanzhong 寰中禅师

Du Jinsheng 都锦生

Empress Dowager Cixi 慈禧太后

Jack Ma (Ma Yun) 马云

Leizu 嫘祖

Louis Cha Leung-yung (Jin Yong)
查良镛（金庸）

Madam Zhao
赵夫人（三国时孙权的夫人）

Mao Yisheng 茅以升

Wang Xingzhai 王星斋

Xie Lingyun 谢灵运

Yellow Emperor 黄帝

Yue Fei 岳飞

Zhu Bingren 朱炳仁

Zhang Xiaoquan 张小泉

Zhu Zhenfei 竹振斐

Books and Brands 书籍与品牌对照表

A Thousand and One Nights
《一千零一夜》

Fuxing Hangluo 福兴杭罗

Kong Feng Chun 孔凤春

The Lotus Sutra 《妙法莲华经》

Wang Xing Ji 王星记

Xidebao 喜得宝

图书在版编目(CIP)数据

杭州一瞥：精编版.摩登时代：英文
蒋景阳主编；王琳，王鉴棋，章晓雯编. — 北京：商务印书馆，
2023
ISBN 978-7-100-22540-3

Ⅰ.①杭… Ⅱ.①蒋… ②王… ③王… ④章… Ⅲ.①英语—语言读物②旅游指南—杭州—英文 Ⅳ.①H319.4：K

中国国家版本馆CIP数据核字(2023)第102975号

版权保留，侵权必究。

杭州一瞥：精编版

蒋景阳 主编

商 务 印 书 馆 出 版
(北京王府井大街36号 邮政编码100710)
商 务 印 书 馆 发 行
北京博海升彩色印刷有限公司印刷
ISBN 978-7-100-22540-3

2023 年 7 月第 1 版	开本 889×1194 1/32
2023 年 7 月第 1 次印刷	印张 7

定价：98.00 元